Honesty: The Foundation for a Meaningful and Fulfilling Life

Tristan

Copyright © [2023]

Author: Tristan

Title: Honesty: The Foundation for a Meaningful and Fulfilling Life

This book is a product of [Publisher's Tristan]

ISBN:

TABLE OF CONTENTS

Chapter 1: The Power of Honesty 08

Chapter 5: Honesty as a Lifestyle Choice   82

Chapter 1: The Power of Honesty

Understanding Honesty

Honesty is a fundamental value that forms the foundation for a meaningful and fulfilling life. In today's fast-paced and complex world, it is easy to lose sight of the importance of being honest. However, honesty is not just about telling the truth; it is a virtue that encompasses integrity, transparency, and trustworthiness. In this subchapter, we will delve into the depths of understanding honesty and its significance in our lives.

Honesty is essential for maintaining healthy relationships and fostering a sense of trust. When we are honest with others, we build a solid foundation for open communication and genuine connections. People are more likely to confide in us, seek our advice, and rely on our support when they know they can trust us to be honest.

Furthermore, honesty is not only about our interactions with others but also with ourselves. Being honest with ourselves means acknowledging our flaws, strengths, and desires. It is about facing the reality of who we are and what we want, without deceiving ourselves or others. This self-awareness allows us to make better decisions, set realistic goals, and live authentically.

Honesty also plays a vital role in personal growth and self-improvement. By being honest about our actions, thoughts, and emotions, we can identify areas where we need to improve or change. It enables us to take responsibility for our actions, learn from our mistakes, and grow as individuals. Honesty is the catalyst for personal development and a stepping stone towards becoming the best version of ourselves.

Additionally, honesty promotes ethical behavior and a sense of integrity. When we prioritize honesty, we are more likely to act in ways that align with our values and principles. Honesty guides us to do what is right, even when it is challenging or inconvenient. It is the compass that keeps us on the path of righteousness and helps us navigate the moral complexities of life.

In conclusion, understanding honesty goes beyond simply telling the truth. It encompasses integrity, transparency, and trustworthiness in our interactions with others and ourselves. The importance of being honest lies in its ability to nurture healthy relationships, foster trust, promote personal growth, and guide us towards ethical behavior. By embracing honesty as a core value, we lay the groundwork for a meaningful and fulfilling life filled with genuine connections, self-awareness, and integrity.

Defining Honesty

Honesty is a fundamental pillar upon which a meaningful and fulfilling life is built. It is an essential quality that every individual should strive to cultivate within themselves. But what exactly does it mean to be honest? In this subchapter, we will delve deeper into the concept of honesty and explore its various dimensions.

At its core, honesty encompasses a commitment to truthfulness and integrity in all aspects of life. It involves being genuine and sincere in our words, actions, and intentions. Honesty means not only speaking the truth but also living it. It requires us to be transparent, authentic, and accountable for our choices and behavior.

In a world often clouded by deception and falsehood, the importance of being honest cannot be overstated. Honesty builds trust and fosters genuine connections with others. It lays the foundation for healthy relationships, both personal and professional. When we are honest, we inspire confidence in others and create an environment where open communication can flourish.

Moreover, honesty is not only about how we interact with others but also about how we relate to ourselves. It involves being honest with our own feelings, desires, and shortcomings. By acknowledging and accepting our true selves, we can embark on a journey of personal growth and self-improvement.

Being honest can sometimes be challenging, especially when faced with difficult decisions or uncomfortable truths. However, the benefits of honesty far outweigh the temporary discomfort it may bring. Honesty allows us to live with integrity, aligning our actions with our values. It liberates us from the burden of deceit and frees our conscience from guilt and regret.

In a society that often glorifies deception and rewards dishonesty, it is crucial to recognize the significance of honesty in our lives. It is not merely a virtue to be admired from a distance but a quality that each one of us can cultivate and embody. By embracing honesty, we can create a world where trust, authenticity, and meaningful connections thrive.

In conclusion, honesty is the cornerstone of a meaningful and fulfilling life. It involves speaking and living the truth, being transparent, and embracing authenticity. Honesty builds trust, fosters genuine connections, and allows for personal growth. It is a quality that each individual can strive to cultivate within themselves, creating a world where honesty is valued and celebrated.

Honesty as a Core Value

In a world that often seems filled with deception and half-truths, honesty is a precious and rare quality. It is a core value that forms the foundation for a meaningful and fulfilling life. Honesty not only shapes our character but also influences our relationships, decisions, and overall well-being. In this subchapter, we will explore the importance of being honest and how it can positively impact every aspect of our lives.

Honesty is the bedrock of trust. When we are honest, we build trust with others, allowing for genuine and authentic connections. Trust is the glue that holds relationships together, whether it be with friends, family, or colleagues. People naturally gravitate towards those who are honest, as they provide a sense of security and reliability. Honesty breeds open communication, fostering understanding, and resolving conflicts effectively. By embracing honesty, we create an environment where trust can thrive, leading to stronger and more fulfilling relationships.

Integrity is another vital aspect of honesty. When we live with integrity, we align our actions with our beliefs and values. It means doing the right thing, even when no one is watching. Integrity builds character and earns the respect of others. We become individuals of integrity by consistently choosing honesty in our daily interactions, maintaining our principles, and upholding ethical standards. It is through integrity that we gain self-respect and the respect of those around us.

Being honest also nourishes personal growth and self-awareness. When we are honest with ourselves, we can acknowledge our strengths and weaknesses, enabling us to learn and grow. Honesty encourages self-reflection, allowing us to identify areas for improvement and take action towards self-improvement. By embracing honesty as a core value, we foster personal growth and develop a deeper understanding of ourselves.

Moreover, honesty has a direct impact on our well-being. Living a life of honesty reduces stress and anxiety. When we are honest, we eliminate the burden of keeping secrets or maintaining false facades. Honesty promotes mental and emotional clarity, allowing us to live with authenticity and peace of mind. By aligning our thoughts, words, and actions with honesty, we cultivate a sense of self-worth and contentment.

In conclusion, honesty is not just a virtue; it is a core value that shapes our lives. It is the key to building trust, fostering meaningful relationships, and maintaining personal integrity. By embracing honesty, we create an environment of authenticity, personal growth, and overall well-being. Let honesty be the guiding principle in your life, and you will find a path to a more meaningful and fulfilling existence.

The Benefits of Honesty

Subchapter: The Benefits of Honesty

In today's fast-paced and complex world, it is easy to lose sight of the importance of being honest. However, honesty remains the foundation for a meaningful and fulfilling life. Whether in personal relationships, professional endeavors, or even in our own self-reflection, honesty plays a pivotal role in shaping our character and the outcomes we experience. In this subchapter, we will explore the numerous benefits that embracing honesty can bring to every aspect of our lives.

First and foremost, honesty builds trust. When we consistently exhibit truthfulness and transparency, we create a solid foundation of trust with those around us. Whether it is our family, friends, or colleagues, trust forms the cornerstone of any successful relationship. Without it, even the strongest bonds can crumble. By being honest, we demonstrate our reliability and integrity, fostering deeper connections and fostering a sense of security and openness with others.

Additionally, honesty promotes personal growth and self-awareness. When we are truthful with ourselves, we are better able to identify our strengths, weaknesses, and areas for improvement. Honesty allows us to confront our flaws and take responsibility for our actions, leading to personal growth and development. By acknowledging our shortcomings and working on them, we can become better versions of ourselves, both in our personal and professional lives.

Moreover, honesty leads to peace of mind. When we are truthful, we eliminate the burden of guilt and the fear of being exposed. Living a life based on lies and deception can be mentally and emotionally draining. On the other hand, being honest allows us to lead a more authentic and genuine life, free from the constant anxiety and stress that dishonesty can bring. It enables us to live with a clear conscience, fostering inner peace and harmony.

In conclusion, the benefits of honesty are far-reaching and encompass every facet of our lives. By embracing honesty, we build trust, foster personal growth, and experience peace of mind. It is a fundamental value that not only shapes our character but also influences the outcomes we achieve. So, let us strive to cultivate a culture of honesty in our interactions, for it is through this virtue that we can create a more meaningful and fulfilling life for ourselves and those around us.

Trust and Authentic Relationships

In a world filled with superficial connections and fleeting interactions, the importance of trust and authentic relationships cannot be emphasized enough. Trust serves as the foundation for building meaningful and fulfilling connections with others, and it is honesty that paves the way towards establishing this trust.

Trust forms the bedrock of any relationship, be it personal or professional. Without trust, relationships become fragile, vulnerable to doubt and suspicion. It is through trust that we feel safe and secure, allowing ourselves to be vulnerable and open with others. Trust is not something that can be demanded or expected; it is earned through honesty and integrity.

Authentic relationships, on the other hand, are built upon a genuine and sincere connection between individuals. In a world where masks and facades are often worn to project a certain image, authentic relationships provide a refreshing respite. They are grounded in honesty, where individuals are true to themselves and others, fostering a deep sense of understanding and acceptance.

Honesty is the cornerstone of trust and authentic relationships. It is the willingness to speak and act truthfully, even when it may be difficult or uncomfortable. Honesty brings transparency to relationships, enabling individuals to know and understand each other on a deeper level. When we are honest with others, we demonstrate respect and integrity, strengthening the bond of trust between us.

Being honest goes beyond just telling the truth; it is about living a life aligned with our values and principles. It means being honest with ourselves, acknowledging our strengths and weaknesses, and taking responsibility for our actions. When we are honest with ourselves, we can then be honest with others, creating an environment conducive to trust and authenticity.

In a world where dishonesty and deceit have become all too common, it is up to each one of us to uphold the importance of being honest. By choosing honesty, we can foster trust and authentic relationships in all aspects of our lives. We can create a ripple effect, inspiring others to do the same and creating a more meaningful and fulfilling world for everyone.

So, let us embrace honesty as the foundation for a meaningful and fulfilling life. Let us cultivate trust and authentic relationships, for it is through these connections that we can truly thrive and find happiness. Remember, honesty is not just a virtue; it is the key that unlocks the door to a more fulfilling existence.

Personal Growth and Self-Discovery

Subchapter: Personal Growth and Self-Discovery

In our journey through life, personal growth and self-discovery are two essential elements that shape us into the individuals we are meant to be. This subchapter delves into the profound impact of honesty on these transformative processes. Regardless of who you are or the particular niche you belong to, embracing the importance of being honest can lead you towards a more meaningful and fulfilling life.

Personal growth is a lifelong process that involves continuous self-improvement and development. It requires us to step out of our comfort zones, challenge our beliefs, and confront our weaknesses. Honesty acts as a catalyst for personal growth, as it encourages us to face the truth about ourselves and the world around us. By being honest with ourselves, we can identify our strengths and weaknesses, paving the way for personal development and improvement. Accepting our flaws and vulnerabilities allows us to embark on a journey of self-improvement, fostering personal growth in all aspects of our lives.

Self-discovery is intimately intertwined with personal growth. It involves exploring our innermost thoughts, desires, and values to gain a deeper understanding of who we truly are. Honesty plays a vital role in self-discovery, as it enables us to be authentic and true to ourselves. By being honest with our feelings, aspirations, and beliefs, we can align our actions with our values, leading to a greater sense of self-fulfillment. Through self-discovery, we uncover our passions and purpose, allowing us to live a more meaningful life.

The importance of being honest extends beyond personal growth and self-discovery. Honesty is the foundation of trust and authenticity in our relationships. It strengthens our connections with others, fostering deeper and more meaningful bonds. By being honest with others, we invite trust, respect, and open communication into our lives. This, in turn, enhances our personal growth and self-discovery, as we learn from the perspectives and experiences of those around us.

In conclusion, personal growth and self-discovery are integral components of a fulfilling life. Honesty serves as the bedrock for these transformative processes, allowing us to confront our weaknesses, embrace our strengths, and live authentically. By understanding the importance of being honest, we can unlock our true potential, cultivate meaningful relationships, and embark on a lifelong journey of self-improvement and self-discovery. Whether you are a student, a professional, a parent, or a retiree, embracing honesty will undoubtedly enrich your life and contribute to your personal growth and self-discovery.

Building a Positive Reputation

In today's fast-paced and interconnected world, the importance of building a positive reputation cannot be overstated. Whether you are a student, a professional, or an entrepreneur, your reputation precedes you and can greatly impact your personal and professional success. Honesty is the foundation for a meaningful and fulfilling life, and it plays a vital role in shaping your reputation.

Being honest is not just about telling the truth; it is about living a life of integrity and authenticity. When you consistently demonstrate honesty in your words and actions, people perceive you as trustworthy and reliable. This, in turn, helps you build strong relationships, both personally and professionally. People are more inclined to work with and support individuals who have a reputation for honesty.

One of the key benefits of building a positive reputation is the increased opportunities that come your way. When others trust you and have confidence in your abilities, they are more likely to recommend you for new opportunities, whether it's a job, a promotion, or a business partnership. Your reputation acts as a powerful endorsement, opening doors that may have otherwise remained closed.

Moreover, a positive reputation also enhances your personal brand. It distinguishes you from the competition and sets you apart as someone who can be relied upon. In a world where first impressions matter, your reputation can make or break your chances of success.

Building a positive reputation starts with consistently practicing honesty in all aspects of your life. Be transparent and truthful in your interactions, whether it is with friends, family, colleagues, or clients. Take responsibility for your actions and admit your mistakes when you make them. Show respect for others and their opinions, even if you disagree. These small acts of honesty and integrity can go a long way in establishing a reputation that others admire and respect.

In conclusion, building a positive reputation is crucial for personal and professional growth. Honesty is the bedrock upon which a reputation is built. By being honest in your words and actions, you can cultivate trust, credibility, and respect. Remember, your reputation is your most valuable asset, and it is up to you to nurture and protect it.

Overcoming the Fear of Honesty

In our journey towards leading a meaningful and fulfilling life, one of the most crucial aspects is the ability to be honest with ourselves and with others. However, for many of us, the fear of honesty can be a significant obstacle that prevents us from experiencing the true power and freedom that comes with living an honest life. In this subchapter, we will explore the fear of honesty and how we can overcome it to create a more authentic and genuine existence.

Being honest is not always easy. It requires vulnerability, self-reflection, and a willingness to confront uncomfortable truths. Many people fear being honest because they worry about the consequences it may bring – the potential for rejection, judgment, or conflict. We may fear that our honesty will be met with negativity or that it will damage our relationships. However, it is important to recognize that honesty is the foundation for all healthy and meaningful connections.

One of the key reasons why honesty is so crucial is that it builds trust. When we are honest with others, we show them that we respect and value them enough to share our true thoughts and feelings. This fosters trust and creates a safe space for open and authentic communication. Without honesty, relationships become superficial and lacking in depth.

To overcome the fear of honesty, it is essential to start by being honest with ourselves. We need to take a deep dive into our emotions, beliefs, and desires, and confront any self-deception or denial that may be holding us back. Self-reflection and introspection allow us to identify our fears and insecurities, helping us to understand why we may have developed a fear of honesty in the first place.

Once we have gained clarity within ourselves, it becomes easier to be honest with others. Start by practicing small acts of honesty, gradually building up to more significant conversations. Remember that being honest does not mean being harsh or hurtful. Honesty can be delivered with compassion and empathy, considering the feelings of others while staying true to our own values.

Overcoming the fear of honesty requires courage and self-awareness. It is a journey of self-discovery that leads to a more meaningful and fulfilling life. By embracing honesty and letting go of our fears, we open ourselves up to deeper connections, personal growth, and a greater sense of authenticity. So, let us embark on this transformative journey together and create a life built on the foundation of honesty.

Identifying the Barriers

In our journey towards leading a meaningful and fulfilling life, honesty serves as a crucial foundation. It shapes our relationships, builds trust, and allows us to stay true to ourselves. However, despite recognizing the importance of being honest, many of us struggle to embrace it fully. To overcome this hurdle, we must first identify the barriers that prevent us from living with utmost honesty and authenticity.

One significant barrier to honesty is fear. We often fear the consequences of being truthful, whether it is the potential for rejection, judgment, or conflict. This fear can be deeply ingrained in our psyche and can paralyze us from expressing our true thoughts and feelings. Overcoming this barrier requires acknowledging that while there may be short-term discomfort, honesty ultimately leads to long-term growth and healthier relationships.

Another barrier lies in the societal pressure to conform. We are often influenced by the expectations and norms imposed upon us by our families, friends, and communities. These external influences can cloud our judgment and make it difficult for us to express our genuine thoughts and values. Recognizing and challenging these societal expectations is crucial in order to live a life that aligns with our true selves.

Furthermore, personal insecurities can act as barriers to honest self-expression. We may fear that our true selves are not good enough or that we will be rejected if we reveal our vulnerabilities. Overcoming these insecurities necessitates cultivating self-compassion and understanding that our worthiness is not determined by external validation, but by our own acceptance and love for ourselves.

Additionally, the fast-paced and demanding nature of modern life can hinder our ability to be honest. We may find ourselves caught up in the chaos, rushing from one task to another, and neglecting to reflect on our thoughts and emotions. Taking the time to slow down, practice mindfulness, and tune into our inner selves can help us identify and address any barriers preventing us from embracing honesty.

Identifying these barriers is the first step towards leading a more honest and authentic life. By recognizing and understanding the fears, societal pressures, personal insecurities, and busy lifestyles that hinder our honesty, we can begin to break free from their grip. With dedication and self-reflection, we can overcome these barriers and create a solid foundation of honesty, paving the way for a more meaningful and fulfilling existence.

Remember, honesty is not just about being truthful to others, but also to ourselves. It is the key to unlocking our full potential, nurturing genuine connections, and living a life that is truly authentic.

Strategies for Overcoming Fear

Fear is a natural emotion that we all experience at some point in our lives. It can be paralyzing, preventing us from pursuing our dreams and living a fulfilling life. However, fear is not something we have to succumb to. With the right strategies, we can overcome our fears and unlock our true potential. In this subchapter, we will explore effective strategies for conquering fear and living a life free from its limitations.

1. Identify the Root Cause: The first step in overcoming fear is to identify its root cause. Take some time to reflect and understand what exactly you are afraid of. Is it failure, rejection, or the unknown? By pinpointing the source of your fear, you can begin to develop strategies to address it.

2. Challenge Your Thoughts: Fear often stems from negative thoughts and beliefs. Challenge those thoughts by questioning their validity. Ask yourself if there is evidence to support your fear or if it is simply a product of your imagination. Replace negative thoughts with positive affirmations and focus on your strengths and abilities.

3. Take Small Steps: Overcoming fear is a gradual process. Start by taking small steps towards facing your fears. Break down your goals into manageable tasks and gradually increase the level of difficulty. Each small step you take will build your confidence and diminish the power of fear.

4. Seek Support: Surround yourself with a supportive network of friends, family, or mentors who can provide encouragement and guidance. Share your fears with them and seek their advice. Sometimes, simply talking about your fears can help alleviate them.

5. Embrace Failure: Fear often stems from the fear of failure. However, it is important to remember that failure is a natural part of the learning process. Embrace failure as an opportunity to grow and learn from your mistakes. Use it as a stepping stone towards success.

6. Practice Mindfulness: Mindfulness is a powerful tool for overcoming fear. By staying present in the moment, you can prevent your mind from wandering into fearful thoughts. Practice deep breathing exercises, meditation, or yoga to cultivate a sense of calm and inner peace.

7. Celebrate Your Successes: As you face and conquer your fears, celebrate your successes, no matter how small they may seem. Acknowledge your progress and reward yourself for your achievements. This positive reinforcement will motivate you to continue pushing past your fears.

Remember, overcoming fear is a journey that requires patience and perseverance. By implementing these strategies into your life, you can slowly but surely break free from the chains of fear and live a meaningful and fulfilling life.

Chapter 2: Honesty in Communication

The Importance of Truthful Communication

In our daily lives, communication plays a vital role in how we interact with others and navigate through various situations. Yet, all too often, we find ourselves veering away from honesty, tempted by the allure of deception or half-truths. However, embracing truthful communication is essential if we seek to build meaningful and fulfilling lives.

At its core, honesty is the foundation upon which trust is built. When we engage in open, sincere, and truthful communication, we foster trust with those around us. Trust forms the bedrock of any healthy relationship, whether it be with family, friends, or colleagues. When we are honest in our interactions, we create an environment where others feel safe to express themselves and share their thoughts and feelings. This leads to deeper connections and stronger bonds, enhancing the quality of our relationships.

Moreover, truthful communication is essential for personal growth and self-awareness. When we are honest with ourselves, we gain a clearer understanding of our strengths, weaknesses, and areas for improvement. This self-awareness allows us to take responsibility for our actions and make positive changes in our lives. By communicating truthfully with others, we invite constructive feedback, enabling us to learn from our mistakes and grow as individuals.

Being honest also promotes authenticity, both in ourselves and in our interactions with others. When we speak the truth, we express our genuine thoughts and emotions, allowing others to see us for who we truly are. This authenticity fosters genuine connections and attracts people who value honesty and integrity. By embracing truthful communication, we create a space where everyone feels comfortable being their authentic selves, leading to more meaningful and fulfilling relationships.

Furthermore, honesty in communication is vital for maintaining a just and equitable society. When we communicate truthfully, we uphold the principles of fairness and justice. By sharing accurate information, we enable others to make informed decisions and take appropriate actions. Truthful communication also helps to prevent the spread of misinformation and deceit, fostering a society built on transparency and accountability.

In conclusion, the importance of truthful communication cannot be overstated. It forms the bedrock of trust, promotes personal growth and authenticity, and contributes to a just and equitable society. By embracing honesty in our interactions, we pave the way for a more meaningful and fulfilling life for ourselves and for those around us.

Building Strong Connections

In today's fast-paced and interconnected world, building strong connections with others has become more important than ever. Whether it's in our personal relationships, friendships, or professional networks, the quality of our connections greatly impacts our overall happiness and fulfillment in life. Honesty, as the foundation for meaningful and fulfilling connections, plays a crucial role in fostering and maintaining these relationships.

Honesty is not only about telling the truth, but also about being authentic and transparent in our interactions with others. When we are honest, we create an environment of trust and openness, where people feel comfortable being themselves. This builds a strong foundation for deeper connections and allows us to truly understand and appreciate one another.

In personal relationships, honesty is paramount. It forms the bedrock of trust and allows for vulnerability and intimacy. When we are honest with our loved ones, we demonstrate our respect and commitment to the relationship. It allows us to address conflicts openly and find solutions together, strengthening the bond between us. Honesty also enables us to set realistic expectations and avoid misunderstandings, reducing the chances of disappointment or resentment.

In friendships, honesty fosters genuine connections. By being honest, we show our friends that we value and trust them. We can share our thoughts, feelings, and fears without fear of judgment or rejection. Honesty helps us build deeper connections based on mutual understanding and acceptance, creating a support system that enriches our lives.

In the professional sphere, honesty is equally crucial. When we are honest in our interactions with colleagues, clients, and superiors, we establish a reputation for integrity and dependability. This builds trust and credibility, leading to stronger professional relationships and increased opportunities for growth and collaboration.

Moreover, honesty also benefits ourselves. When we are honest with ourselves, we can identify our strengths and weaknesses, allowing us to grow and improve. It enables us to make better decisions and align our actions with our values, leading to a more fulfilling and purpose-driven life.

In conclusion, building strong connections is essential for a meaningful and fulfilling life. Honesty serves as the foundation for these connections, fostering trust, understanding, and authenticity. Whether in personal relationships, friendships, or professional networks, honesty plays a vital role in creating lasting and enriching connections. By embracing honesty, we not only strengthen our relationships with others but also cultivate a deeper connection with ourselves.

Fostering Openness and Vulnerability

In a world that often celebrates strength and invulnerability, fostering openness and vulnerability may seem counterintuitive. However, in the pursuit of a meaningful and fulfilling life, these qualities are not only important but crucial. By embracing openness and vulnerability, we can experience deeper connections, personal growth, and a greater sense of authenticity.

Openness is the key to unlocking the doors of understanding and empathy. When we are open, we allow ourselves to truly listen and engage with others, without judgment or preconceived notions. This level of openness enables us to see different perspectives, challenge our own beliefs, and foster a sense of unity and connectedness. By embracing openness, we create a safe space for others to share their thoughts and feelings, encouraging honest and meaningful conversations that lead to personal growth and collective progress.

Vulnerability, on the other hand, may be perceived as a weakness, but it is, in fact, a tremendous strength. When we allow ourselves to be vulnerable, we acknowledge our humanity and our limitations. This act of courage opens the door to authentic connections and genuine relationships. By being vulnerable, we invite others to reciprocate, creating an environment of trust and understanding where true emotional intimacy can flourish. It is through vulnerability that we can truly be seen and accepted for who we are, leading to a profound sense of fulfillment and self-acceptance.

In the pursuit of a meaningful and fulfilling life, honesty is the foundation upon which all other virtues are built. Without honesty, openness and vulnerability are impossible to achieve. Honesty is not just about telling the truth, but also about being truthful to ourselves and others in every aspect of our lives. It is about facing our fears, acknowledging our mistakes, and taking responsibility for our actions. When we are honest, we cultivate integrity and authenticity, both of which are essential for personal growth and building strong, meaningful relationships.

By fostering openness and vulnerability, we create a space where honesty can flourish. We allow ourselves and others to be seen in our truest form, embracing imperfections and celebrating our shared humanity. This openness not only strengthens our relationships but also enriches our own lives, as it encourages personal growth and self-reflection. Through the power of honesty, openness, and vulnerability, we can pave the way for a more meaningful and fulfilling existence, both individually and collectively.

So, let us all strive to foster openness and vulnerability in our lives. Let us embrace the power of honesty and create a world where genuine connections and authentic relationships are the norm. By doing so, we will unlock the true potential of our lives, and experience a depth of fulfillment and meaning that can only be achieved through openness, vulnerability, and honesty.

Practicing Honest Communication

In a world where deception and dishonesty seem to be prevalent, practicing honest communication has become more crucial than ever. Honesty is not just about telling the truth; it is about embodying integrity, authenticity, and transparency in all aspects of our lives. From personal relationships to professional interactions, practicing honest communication lays the foundation for a meaningful and fulfilling life.

One of the key aspects of honest communication is the importance of being truthful with ourselves. It requires a deep sense of self-awareness and the willingness to acknowledge our flaws, mistakes, and limitations. When we are honest with ourselves, we can better understand our values, desires, and aspirations. This self-awareness forms the basis for authentic communication with others.

Being honest in our communication with others fosters trust and strengthens relationships. When we speak truthfully, we demonstrate respect for others' feelings and beliefs. Honest communication builds a solid foundation of trust, allowing for open and genuine connections. It enables us to express our thoughts and emotions sincerely, leading to deeper and more meaningful relationships.

Practicing honest communication also promotes personal growth and development. When we are honest with ourselves and others, we create an environment that encourages self-reflection and learning. Honest feedback and constructive criticism help us identify areas for improvement and allows us to make necessary changes. It also helps us build resilience and emotional intelligence, as we learn to handle difficult conversations with grace and empathy.

In the professional realm, honest communication is vital for success. Employers value employees who are honest and trustworthy, as it fosters a positive and collaborative work environment. Honest communication in the workplace leads to increased productivity, better problem-solving, and effective teamwork. It allows for open dialogue and innovation, as employees feel safe to express their ideas and concerns without fear of judgment or retribution.

In conclusion, practicing honest communication is essential for everyone, regardless of their background or profession. It forms the foundation for a meaningful and fulfilling life, fostering trust, personal growth, and strong relationships. By being honest with ourselves and others, we create an environment that encourages authenticity, transparency, and open communication. Let us embrace the power of honest communication and strive to build a world where integrity and truthfulness are valued and celebrated.

Active Listening and Empathy

Subchapter: Active Listening and Empathy

Introduction:
In our fast-paced world, filled with distractions and constant noise, it has become increasingly challenging to truly connect with others. However, the ability to actively listen and empathize with those around us is crucial for building meaningful relationships. In this subchapter, we will explore the importance of active listening and empathy in our daily lives, and how they contribute to our overall honesty and fulfillment.

The Power of Active Listening:
Active listening goes beyond simply hearing the words someone is saying. It involves giving our full attention, understanding their perspective, and responding with genuine interest. By actively listening, we create a safe and nurturing environment where others feel valued and validated. This allows for open and honest communication, leading to stronger connections with our loved ones, colleagues, and even strangers.

Empathy: The Key to Understanding:
Empathy is the ability to understand and share the feelings of another person. It is the foundation for compassion and genuine concern for others. By putting ourselves in someone else's shoes, we gain a deeper insight into their experiences, thoughts, and emotions. This understanding allows us to respond with kindness, respect, and integrity, fostering an environment of honesty and trust.

Benefits of Active Listening and Empathy: By practicing active listening and empathy, we not only strengthen our relationships but also enhance our own personal growth. We learn to suspend judgment, become more open-minded, and develop a broader perspective. Active listening and empathy enable us to create a space where others feel safe to express themselves authentically, leading to more meaningful and fulfilling interactions.

Applying Active Listening and Empathy in Daily Life: To become better active listeners and cultivate empathy, we must first silence the inner chatter and distractions that hinder our ability to connect. We can start by making a conscious effort to be fully present in conversations, maintaining eye contact, and avoiding interrupting or formulating responses prematurely. It is also essential to practice empathy by actively seeking to understand others' viewpoints, asking clarifying questions, and validating their emotions.

Conclusion:
Active listening and empathy are powerful tools that enhance our ability to connect with others on a deeper level. By practicing these skills, we can foster an environment of honesty, trust, and respect, leading to more meaningful and fulfilling relationships. In a world that often values speed and efficiency over genuine connection, let us strive to be the ones who listen with intent, understand with empathy, and build a more honest and fulfilling life for ourselves and those around us.

Assertiveness and Speaking Truthfully

Assertiveness and speaking truthfully are crucial aspects of living an honest and fulfilling life. In today's world, where dishonesty and deception seem to have become the norm, it is more important than ever to understand the significance of being honest and assertive in our communication.

Being assertive means expressing our thoughts, feelings, and beliefs in a clear and respectful manner, without being aggressive or passive. It involves standing up for ourselves and our values, while also respecting the rights and opinions of others. When we are assertive, we communicate honestly and effectively, which fosters healthy relationships and builds trust.

Speaking truthfully is an integral part of assertiveness. It means being honest and transparent in our words, actions, and intentions. When we speak truthfully, we avoid misleading others or bending the truth to suit our own interests. Instead, we strive for authenticity and integrity in our communication.

One of the reasons why assertiveness and speaking truthfully are so important is that they lay the foundation for meaningful and fulfilling relationships. When we are honest with ourselves and others, we create an environment of trust and openness. We allow others to see and accept us for who we truly are, and we give ourselves the opportunity to be understood and respected.

Moreover, assertiveness and speaking truthfully help us avoid unnecessary conflicts and misunderstandings. By expressing our needs, desires, and boundaries honestly, we prevent resentment and frustration from building up. We also encourage others to do the same, promoting open and honest communication that leads to healthier relationships.

In addition, being assertive and speaking truthfully empower us to make better decisions and take control of our lives. When we are honest with ourselves about our strengths, weaknesses, and desires, we can set realistic goals and make choices that align with our values. We become more confident in expressing our needs and asserting our boundaries, leading to greater self-esteem and personal growth.

In conclusion, assertiveness and speaking truthfully are essential for living an honest and fulfilling life. By being assertive, we communicate effectively and build trust in our relationships. Speaking truthfully allows us to be authentic and transparent, fostering understanding and respect. These qualities not only enhance our personal lives but also contribute to a more honest and compassionate society.

Honesty in Conflict Resolution

Conflict is an inevitable part of human interaction. Whether it's a disagreement with a loved one, a heated debate with a colleague, or a clash of opinions in a social setting, conflicts can arise in various aspects of our lives. However, the way we handle these conflicts speaks volumes about our character and the quality of our relationships. This subchapter, titled "Honesty in Conflict Resolution," delves into the importance of being honest when resolving conflicts and how it serves as a foundation for a meaningful and fulfilling life.

At the core of honesty in conflict resolution lies the principle of authenticity. Honesty allows us to express our true feelings and opinions without fear of judgment or rejection. By being honest, we create an open and safe space for dialogue, enabling a deeper understanding of each other's perspectives. This openness fosters empathy and compassion, which are vital in resolving conflicts in a fair and respectful manner.

When we approach conflict resolution with honesty, we also establish trust. Trust is the bedrock of any healthy relationship, be it personal or professional. By being honest about our intentions and motivations, we show others that we value their trust and are committed to finding mutually beneficial solutions. Trust allows us to establish common ground, build bridges, and move forward together, even after a conflict.

Moreover, honesty in conflict resolution promotes personal growth. By honestly reflecting on our own actions and taking responsibility for our mistakes, we can learn from our conflicts and develop a better understanding of ourselves. This self-awareness helps us recognize patterns of behavior that may contribute to conflicts and enables us to make positive changes. Honesty also encourages us to listen actively and consider others' perspectives, broadening our horizons and fostering personal growth.

In conclusion, honesty is a crucial element in conflict resolution. By being honest, we establish authenticity, trust, and personal growth. It allows us to navigate conflicts with integrity and respect, paving the way for meaningful and fulfilling relationships. Whether in our personal lives or professional endeavors, embracing honesty in conflict resolution can lead to a more harmonious and satisfying existence. Remember, being honest doesn't mean being hurtful; it means expressing ourselves truthfully while considering the feelings and perspectives of others. Let honesty be the compass that guides you through conflicts, and watch as it transforms your relationships and your life.

Constructive Feedback and Criticism

In the journey of living a meaningful and fulfilling life, one of the key virtues we must cultivate is honesty. Honesty not only allows us to build trust and maintain healthy relationships, but it also enables personal growth and development. As we navigate through the various aspects of life, it becomes crucial to understand the significance of constructive feedback and criticism.

Constructive feedback and criticism play a vital role in our personal and professional growth. They provide us with valuable insights and perspectives that can help us improve ourselves and our work. However, receiving feedback can be challenging, as it often involves hearing about our shortcomings or areas that need improvement. Nevertheless, when approached with an open mind and a willingness to learn, feedback can be a powerful tool for self-improvement.

One of the first steps in receiving constructive feedback is to cultivate a growth mindset. Understand that feedback is not a personal attack but an opportunity for growth. Embrace the idea that feedback helps you become better, and view it as a gift rather than a criticism. By adopting this mindset, you create a safe space for others to provide honest feedback without fear of hurting your feelings.

Additionally, it is important to actively seek feedback rather than waiting for others to offer it. By proactively seeking feedback, you demonstrate your commitment to personal growth, and it also allows you to gain different perspectives that you may have overlooked. This can be done by asking specific questions or requesting feedback on specific areas where you want to improve.

When receiving feedback, it is essential to listen actively and non-defensively. Avoid becoming defensive or making excuses for your actions. Instead, truly listen to what the other person is saying, and take the time to reflect on their insights. Remember, feedback is an opportunity for growth, and by being open to it, you can uncover blind spots and make positive changes in your life.

Lastly, after receiving feedback, take action. Use the feedback you receive as a roadmap for improvement. Implement the necessary changes and continually assess your progress. Remember that personal growth is a lifelong journey, and feedback serves as a valuable guide along the way.

In conclusion, constructive feedback and criticism are essential elements in our pursuit of a meaningful and fulfilling life. By embracing feedback with a growth mindset, actively seeking it, listening non-defensively, and taking action, we can harness the power of feedback to become the best version of ourselves. Let us remember that the importance of being honest extends beyond just telling the truth but also in embracing feedback as a catalyst for personal growth and development.

Mediation and Reconciliation

In the pursuit of leading a meaningful and fulfilling life, one cannot overlook the significance of mediation and reconciliation. These two practices hold the power to heal relationships, restore harmony, and foster a deep sense of understanding and empathy among individuals. In this subchapter, we will explore how mediation and reconciliation contribute to the overall importance of being honest.

To begin, let us acknowledge that conflicts and disagreements are an inevitable part of human interaction. Whether it is in our personal relationships, workplaces, or communities, we are bound to encounter situations where honesty is called upon to resolve disputes. This is where mediation steps in as a valuable tool. Mediation involves the intervention of a neutral third party who facilitates communication and negotiation between conflicting parties. By encouraging open and honest dialogue, mediation allows individuals to express their grievances, listen to one another's perspectives, and work towards a mutually satisfactory solution.

Through the process of mediation, not only do individuals find resolutions to their conflicts, but they also develop a deeper understanding of themselves and others. They learn to empathize, to see beyond their own biases, and to appreciate the diverse experiences and viewpoints that shape human interactions. In this way, mediation becomes a catalyst for personal growth and the cultivation of meaningful relationships.

However, it is important to acknowledge that not all conflicts can be easily resolved through mediation alone. This is where the concept of reconciliation comes into play. Reconciliation involves a deeper level of healing, forgiveness, and acceptance. It requires individuals to let go of past grievances, acknowledge their own shortcomings, and embrace the possibility of a renewed relationship.

Reconciliation is a profound act of honesty as it compels individuals to confront their own vulnerabilities and take responsibility for their actions. It requires humility, empathy, and a genuine desire to restore trust and harmony. By engaging in the process of reconciliation, individuals not only mend broken relationships but also nurture a culture of honesty, compassion, and forgiveness.

In conclusion, mediation and reconciliation are powerful tools in the pursuit of a meaningful and fulfilling life. They enable us to address conflicts with honesty, openness, and empathy. Through mediation, we develop the skills necessary to navigate disagreements, while reconciliation allows us to heal and restore relationships that have been damaged. By embracing these practices, we create a foundation of honesty that fosters personal growth, strengthens connections, and ultimately leads to a more meaningful and fulfilling life for everyone.

Chapter 3: Honesty with Oneself

Self-Reflection and Personal Growth

In our fast-paced modern world, it is easy to get caught up in the hustle and bustle of everyday life. We often find ourselves rushing from one task to another, barely taking a moment to pause and reflect on our own personal growth. However, self-reflection is an essential practice that can lead to a more meaningful and fulfilling life.

Self-reflection is the process of looking inward and examining our thoughts, feelings, and actions. It allows us to gain a deeper understanding of ourselves, our values, and our goals. By taking the time to reflect, we can identify areas for improvement and make positive changes in our lives.

Personal growth is closely linked to self-reflection. When we engage in self-reflection, we become aware of our strengths and weaknesses. This self-awareness is the first step towards personal growth. It allows us to build on our strengths and work on developing areas that need improvement.

Honesty plays a crucial role in self-reflection and personal growth. Being honest with ourselves means facing our flaws and shortcomings head-on. It means acknowledging our mistakes and taking responsibility for them. Honesty allows us to learn from our experiences and grow as individuals.

The importance of being honest cannot be overstated. When we are honest with ourselves, we create a solid foundation for personal growth. We can identify patterns of behavior that may be holding us back and make necessary changes. Honesty also fosters self-acceptance and self-love, as we learn to embrace all aspects of ourselves, both positive and negative.

Self-reflection and personal growth are ongoing processes. It is important to set aside time regularly to reflect on our thoughts, feelings, and actions. This can be done through journaling, meditation, or engaging in meaningful conversations with trusted friends or mentors.

By dedicating ourselves to self-reflection and personal growth, we can unlock our true potential and live a more meaningful and fulfilling life. It is through this journey of self-discovery that we can cultivate a deeper sense of purpose and find true happiness. So, let us embark on this transformative journey of self-reflection and personal growth, guided by the principles of honesty and authenticity.

Recognizing Our Strengths and Weaknesses

In our journey towards leading a meaningful and fulfilling life, it is crucial to take a step back and evaluate ourselves honestly. Understanding our strengths and weaknesses is a fundamental aspect of personal growth, as it allows us to make informed decisions, set realistic goals, and build upon our strengths to overcome our weaknesses. This subchapter aims to explore the significance of recognizing our strengths and weaknesses and how it contributes to the importance of being honest.

Firstly, recognizing our strengths provides us with a solid foundation upon which we can build our lives. Each one of us possesses unique talents, skills, and qualities that make us special. By acknowledging and embracing these strengths, we gain the confidence and motivation needed to excel in various aspects of our lives. Moreover, recognizing our strengths allows us to identify opportunities where we can utilize them to make a positive impact on ourselves and the world around us.

However, it is equally important to acknowledge our weaknesses. Our weaknesses are not something to be ashamed of; they are simply areas where we have room for improvement. By honestly recognizing our weaknesses, we can work towards strengthening and overcoming them. This self-awareness helps us avoid situations where our weaknesses might hinder our progress and enables us to seek support or acquire new skills to compensate for them.

Being honest about our strengths and weaknesses also fosters genuine and meaningful relationships. When we are open and transparent about who we are, we invite others to do the same. This mutual honesty creates an atmosphere of trust and understanding, allowing for deeper connections and more authentic interactions. Furthermore, recognizing and accepting our own weaknesses helps us show empathy and compassion towards others, as we understand that everyone has their own struggles and imperfections.

In conclusion, recognizing our strengths and weaknesses is an essential part of our personal development and contributes significantly to the importance of being honest. By honestly evaluating ourselves, we can harness our strengths to achieve our goals, work on our weaknesses to grow and improve, and build stronger relationships with those around us. Embracing our strengths and weaknesses allows us to live a more authentic and fulfilling life, leading us towards a brighter and more meaningful future.

Embracing Vulnerability and Authenticity

In our journey towards leading a meaningful and fulfilling life, there is one crucial aspect that often goes unnoticed: vulnerability and authenticity. These two qualities are the foundation of true honesty and can have a profound impact on our relationships, personal growth, and overall well-being. In this subchapter, we will explore the significance of embracing vulnerability and authenticity, and how they contribute to living a more honest and fulfilling life.

Vulnerability, contrary to popular belief, is not a weakness, but rather a strength. It is the willingness to expose our true selves, flaws and all, to others. When we allow ourselves to be vulnerable, we open the door for genuine connections and deepen our relationships. By showing our vulnerabilities, we create an environment of trust and empathy, allowing others to feel comfortable in reciprocating their own vulnerabilities. In doing so, we foster authentic and meaningful connections that enrich our lives.

Authenticity is closely intertwined with vulnerability. It is about living in alignment with our true selves, rather than putting on a façade to please others or conform to societal expectations. When we embrace authenticity, we bring forth our unique perspectives, talents, and passions. We are no longer bound by the fear of judgment or rejection, as we understand that our true worth lies in being genuine. By embracing our authentic selves, we open up doors to self-discovery, personal growth, and a sense of fulfillment that cannot be achieved when living a life based on pretense.

The importance of being honest cannot be overstated. When we embrace vulnerability and authenticity, we create an environment conducive to honesty. By being honest with ourselves and others, we foster trust, build stronger relationships, and live a life of integrity. Honesty allows us to acknowledge and address our shortcomings, learn from our mistakes, and grow as individuals. It is the key to living a life that is aligned with our values and purpose.

To truly embrace vulnerability and authenticity, we must learn to let go of the fear of judgment and rejection. It requires courage to be vulnerable and authentic, but the rewards far outweigh the risks. By embracing these qualities, we invite more love, connection, and fulfillment into our lives. So, let us embark on this journey together, to live a life that is honest, meaningful, and authentic.

Honesty in Setting Goals

Setting goals is an integral part of leading a meaningful and fulfilling life. It provides a sense of direction and purpose, allowing us to make the most of our abilities and potential. However, the path to achieving our goals can be fraught with challenges and temptations that may test our commitment and integrity. This is where honesty in setting goals becomes crucial.

Being honest with ourselves is the first step towards setting meaningful goals. It requires a deep introspection and a clear understanding of our values, strengths, and weaknesses. When we are honest about what truly matters to us, we can set goals that align with our authentic selves, rather than succumbing to societal expectations or pursuing goals that offer short-term gratification.

Honesty also plays a crucial role in setting realistic goals. It is important to acknowledge our limitations and be truthful about what we can realistically achieve within a given timeframe. Setting unrealistic goals can lead to disappointment, frustration, and a loss of motivation. By being honest about our capabilities and resources, we can set achievable goals that inspire us to strive for excellence while maintaining a healthy balance in our lives.

Furthermore, honesty in goal-setting fosters a sense of accountability. By openly acknowledging our intentions and aspirations, we invite others to support us on our journey. This accountability ensures that we stay on track and remain committed to our goals, even when faced with obstacles or setbacks. Additionally, being honest about our progress allows us to evaluate and adjust our goals as needed, ensuring that they remain relevant and attainable.

Finally, honesty in setting goals cultivates a sense of integrity and authenticity. When we set goals that are in line with our values and aspirations, we are more likely to approach them with enthusiasm and dedication. This authenticity not only enhances our motivation but also attracts opportunities and resources that align with our goals, creating a positive ripple effect in our lives.

In conclusion, honesty in setting goals is essential for leading a meaningful and fulfilling life. By being honest with ourselves about our values, capabilities, and aspirations, we can set realistic and authentic goals that inspire us to reach our full potential. This honesty also fosters accountability, ensuring that we stay committed to our goals and make necessary adjustments along the way. Let us embrace honesty in goal-setting and pave the way for a truly meaningful and fulfilling life.

Aligning Goals with Personal Values

In today's fast-paced and competitive world, it is easy to get caught up in the pursuit of success without considering how our goals align with our personal values. However, living a meaningful and fulfilling life requires us to be honest with ourselves and ensure that our goals are in alignment with our core values.

Understanding the importance of being honest with ourselves is the first step towards achieving true happiness and fulfillment. When we are honest about our values, we gain clarity and direction in our lives. We are able to set goals that are meaningful to us and bring us closer to our authentic selves.

Aligning our goals with our personal values is essential for several reasons. Firstly, it ensures that we are pursuing goals that truly matter to us. When our goals align with our values, we are more motivated, focused, and passionate about achieving them. This helps us overcome obstacles and setbacks along the way, as our values serve as a guiding force in our journey.

Moreover, aligning goals with personal values leads to a greater sense of authenticity and integrity. When we set goals that are in line with our values, we are being true to ourselves and living in accordance with our beliefs. This authenticity radiates through our actions and interactions, creating deeper and more meaningful connections with others.

Additionally, aligning goals with personal values enhances our overall well-being. When we are pursuing goals that align with our values, we experience a sense of fulfillment and satisfaction. We are more likely to experience a state of flow, where time seems to fly by and we are fully engaged in the present moment. This state of flow brings about a sense of joy and contentment, ultimately leading to a more meaningful life.

To align goals with personal values, it is important to reflect on our core beliefs and values. Take time to identify what truly matters to you and what you want to prioritize in your life. Evaluate your current goals and determine if they are in alignment with your values. If not, consider making necessary adjustments or setting new goals that are more in tune with your values.

Remember, aligning goals with personal values is an ongoing process. As we grow and evolve, our values might change, and our goals should reflect these changes. Regularly reassessing our goals and ensuring they align with our values is crucial for maintaining a meaningful and fulfilling life.

In conclusion, aligning goals with personal values is vital for living a meaningful and fulfilling life. Being honest with ourselves about our values allows us to set goals that truly matter to us and bring us closer to our authentic selves. It leads to a greater sense of authenticity, integrity, and overall well-being. By aligning our goals with our personal values, we can create a life that is not only successful but also deeply fulfilling and meaningful.

Overcoming Self-Deception and Rationalization

Self-deception and rationalization are powerful defense mechanisms that we all use to protect ourselves from uncomfortable truths. In our pursuit of honesty and living a meaningful life, it is crucial to recognize and overcome these barriers. This subchapter explores the significance of overcoming self-deception and rationalization, providing practical strategies for embracing a more honest and fulfilling existence.

Self-deception is a tricky mental process where we convince ourselves of something that is not true, often to avoid facing reality. It can occur in various aspects of our lives, from personal relationships to professional endeavors. Recognizing self-deception requires a willingness to confront our own biases, fears, and insecurities. By acknowledging our tendency to deceive ourselves, we can begin to unravel the layers of falsehood and embrace a more authentic existence.

Rationalization, on the other hand, is the process of justifying our actions or beliefs, even when they contradict our values or the truth. It allows us to create excuses or explanations that shield us from the discomfort of acknowledging our mistakes or flaws. Overcoming rationalization involves developing the ability to critically examine our thoughts and actions, challenging our own justifications, and accepting responsibility for our choices.

By overcoming self-deception and rationalization, we can unlock the true power of honesty in our lives. Honesty brings forth authenticity, allowing us to align our actions with our values and live in integrity. It fosters genuine connections with others, as people are naturally drawn to those who are honest and trustworthy.

Embracing honesty also liberates us from the burden of guilt and shame. When we deceive ourselves or rationalize our actions, we often carry a sense of unease or internal conflict. By confronting the truth, we can let go of these negative emotions and experience a greater sense of inner peace.

To overcome self-deception and rationalization, it is essential to cultivate self-awareness. This involves regularly reflecting on our thoughts, feelings, and behaviors, and questioning our motives and intentions. Seeking feedback from trusted individuals can also provide valuable insights into our blind spots.

Furthermore, practicing mindfulness can help us observe our thoughts without judgment, allowing us to recognize when we are deceiving ourselves or rationalizing our actions. By developing a non-judgmental attitude towards ourselves, we can create a safe space for honesty and growth.

In conclusion, overcoming self-deception and rationalization is pivotal to living a meaningful and fulfilling life. By embracing honesty, we can break free from the confines of deceit and rationalization, fostering authenticity, genuine connections, and inner peace. Developing self-awareness and practicing mindfulness are essential tools on this journey. Let us embark on this path towards a more honest existence, where truth and integrity shape our every action.

Cultivating Self-Trust

In our journey towards leading an honest and meaningful life, one of the most crucial aspects we must focus on is cultivating self-trust. Self-trust goes hand in hand with honesty, as it is the foundation upon which our integrity and authenticity are built. When we trust ourselves, we are better equipped to navigate life's challenges, make sound decisions, and maintain healthy relationships.

Self-trust is not something that can be developed overnight. It requires a conscious effort and continuous practice. However, the rewards of cultivating self-trust are immeasurable. When we trust ourselves, we become more confident in our abilities and more resilient in the face of adversity. We no longer second-guess our decisions or constantly seek validation from others. Instead, we rely on our own judgment and intuition, knowing that we have the wisdom and integrity to make the right choices.

To cultivate self-trust, we must start by being honest with ourselves. This means acknowledging our strengths and weaknesses, accepting our mistakes, and taking responsibility for our actions. Honesty allows us to confront our own flaws and work towards personal growth. It is through this introspection that we can truly understand who we are and what we stand for.

Another important aspect of cultivating self-trust is setting realistic expectations for ourselves. Often, we fall into the trap of comparing ourselves to others or succumbing to societal pressures. However, true self-trust comes from recognizing our own unique talents and capabilities. By setting attainable goals and celebrating our successes, no matter how small, we build a strong foundation of self-trust.

Furthermore, self-care plays a crucial role in cultivating self-trust. Taking care of our physical, emotional, and mental well-being allows us to be in tune with ourselves and make decisions that align with our values. Engaging in activities that bring us joy, practicing mindfulness, and surrounding ourselves with positive influences are all essential components of self-care that contribute to building self-trust.

In conclusion, cultivating self-trust is a vital step on the path towards leading an honest and meaningful life. By being honest with ourselves, setting realistic expectations, and practicing self-care, we lay the groundwork for building a strong sense of self-trust. This self-trust empowers us to make authentic choices, maintain healthy relationships, and navigate life's challenges with confidence. Remember, self-trust is not an end goal but a continuous journey of self-discovery and growth. Embrace it, nurture it, and let it guide you towards a more fulfilling and authentic life.

Honoring Commitments and Promises

In our journey through life, one of the most fundamental aspects of living a meaningful and fulfilling life is honoring commitments and promises. Being honest and true to our word is not only a virtue but also a cornerstone of building trust and maintaining healthy relationships with others. In this subchapter, we will delve into the significance of honoring our commitments and promises, exploring the profound impact it has on our personal growth, professional success, and overall well-being.

At its core, honoring commitments and promises is about integrity. When we make a commitment or promise, whether it is to ourselves or others, we are essentially making a pact to follow through and deliver on that commitment. By doing so, we demonstrate our reliability and trustworthiness, which in turn strengthens the bond of trust with those around us.

In our personal lives, honoring commitments and promises is crucial for fostering healthy relationships. Whether it is keeping a promise to spend quality time with our loved ones, being there for a friend in need, or fulfilling obligations within our community, our actions speak volumes about our character. When we consistently honor our commitments, we build a reputation for being dependable and trustworthy, which ultimately leads to deeper connections and a sense of belonging.

Moreover, in the professional realm, honoring commitments and promises is paramount for success. Employers value employees who demonstrate reliability and dedication to their work. By consistently meeting deadlines, delivering on promises, and fulfilling obligations, we not only enhance our professional reputation but also create opportunities for growth and advancement.

Beyond personal and professional relationships, honoring commitments and promises has a profound impact on our own self-esteem and sense of fulfillment. When we follow through on our commitments, we build a sense of personal integrity and self-trust. This, in turn, boosts our confidence and allows us to take on new challenges and pursue our goals with determination.

In conclusion, honoring commitments and promises is not just a moral obligation, but also a key ingredient for leading a meaningful and fulfilling life. By being honest and true to our word, we build trust in our relationships, enhance our professional reputation, and nurture our own self-esteem. So, let us strive to be individuals who honor commitments and promises, as it is through this practice that we can truly create a life filled with purpose, happiness, and success.

Learning from Mistakes and Taking Responsibility

Mistakes are an inevitable part of life. We all make them, regardless of age, gender, or background. However, what truly matters is how we respond to these mistakes and the level of responsibility we take for our actions. In this subchapter, we will explore the significance of learning from our mistakes and the importance of taking responsibility for our choices.

One of the greatest lessons we can learn from mistakes is that they provide us with valuable opportunities for growth and self-improvement. When we make a mistake, it is crucial to reflect on what went wrong and analyze the factors that contributed to it. By doing so, we gain insight into our weaknesses and areas for improvement. This self-reflection helps us avoid repeating the same mistakes in the future and empowers us to make better choices.

Taking responsibility for our mistakes is equally important. It means acknowledging our role in the outcome and not shying away from the consequences. When we take responsibility, we demonstrate integrity and honesty, traits that are essential for building trust and meaningful relationships. Moreover, accepting responsibility allows us to learn from our mistakes and make amends if necessary. It shows maturity and a willingness to grow as individuals.

However, taking responsibility is not always easy. It requires humility and a willingness to admit our faults and shortcomings. It may involve apologizing to those we have hurt or affected by our actions. Yet, by doing so, we open the door for healing and reconciliation, both with ourselves and others.

Learning from mistakes and taking responsibility also serves as a powerful example for those around us. When we are honest about our mistakes and show accountability, we inspire others to do the same. In a world where dishonesty and blame-shifting are prevalent, being a beacon of integrity can have a profound impact on our communities and society as a whole.

In conclusion, learning from mistakes and taking responsibility is an essential aspect of leading a meaningful and fulfilling life. It allows us to grow, become better versions of ourselves, and build strong relationships based on trust and honesty. By embracing our mistakes and accepting responsibility, we not only create opportunities for personal growth but also inspire others to do the same. Let us remember that mistakes are not failures but stepping stones towards a brighter and more authentic future.

Chapter 4: Honesty in Relationships

Building Trust in Intimate Relationships

In the pursuit of a meaningful and fulfilling life, one cannot overlook the crucial role that honesty plays in cultivating strong and lasting intimate relationships. Whether you are in a committed partnership, engaged in dating, or looking for that special someone, trust is the bedrock upon which these connections are built. This subchapter delves into the significance of building trust in intimate relationships and how honesty serves as the foundation for fostering a deep and meaningful bond.

Trust is the cornerstone of any successful relationship, as it creates a safe space for vulnerability, open communication, and emotional intimacy. When we are honest with our partners, we allow them to truly know us and accept us for who we are. This vulnerability paves the way for a deeper connection and understanding, fostering an environment in which both individuals can grow and flourish.

However, building trust is not a one-time endeavor; it is a continuous process that requires intention, effort, and consistency. Honesty must be practiced not only in the big moments but also in the small everyday interactions. By consistently being truthful, even in the face of potential discomfort or conflict, we demonstrate our commitment to the relationship and build a solid foundation of trust.

It is important to note that honesty goes beyond simply avoiding lies or deceit. It also encompasses transparency, authenticity, and accountability. When we are transparent about our thoughts, feelings, and intentions, we invite our partners into our world, creating a space where trust can thrive. Authenticity allows for genuine connection, as we show up as our true selves, rather than putting on a façade. Furthermore, taking responsibility for our actions and being accountable for the impact they have on our partners is crucial for maintaining trust.

In a world where dishonesty and betrayal have become all too common, it is paramount to prioritize the importance of being honest in our intimate relationships. By doing so, we not only build trust but also cultivate a sense of security, emotional safety, and mutual respect. These qualities enable both individuals to feel valued, understood, and cherished, creating a strong foundation for a meaningful and fulfilling life together.

In conclusion, building trust in intimate relationships is a fundamental aspect of fostering a meaningful and fulfilling life. Through honesty, transparency, authenticity, and accountability, we create a safe space for vulnerability, open communication, and emotional intimacy. By prioritizing the importance of being honest in our relationships, we lay the groundwork for a deep and lasting connection that allows both individuals to grow and thrive together.

Open Communication and Transparency

In our journey towards leading a meaningful and fulfilling life, one fundamental principle that cannot be overlooked is open communication and transparency. Honest and open communication serves as the cornerstone for building trust, fostering healthy relationships, and achieving personal growth. It is a vital aspect that applies to every one of us, regardless of our background, profession, or age.

The importance of being honest cannot be overstated. When we communicate openly and truthfully, we create an environment that encourages trust and authenticity. This environment enables us to connect with others on a deeper level, leading to more meaningful relationships. Open communication allows us to express our thoughts, feelings, and concerns honestly, enabling others to understand us better and vice versa. By embracing honesty, we can build a solid foundation for lasting relationships, be it in our personal or professional lives.

Transparency plays a crucial role in our personal growth and development. When we are transparent with ourselves and others, we create an opportunity for self-reflection and introspection. By acknowledging our strengths and weaknesses, we can work towards self-improvement and become more effective in our interactions. Transparency also fosters a culture of accountability, where we take responsibility for our actions and decisions. This cultivates a sense of integrity and reliability, which are highly valued traits in any setting.

In the professional realm, open communication and transparency are essential for effective teamwork and collaboration. By openly sharing information and ideas, we create an environment that encourages innovation and problem-solving. When team members are transparent with each other, it fosters trust and promotes a sense of collective responsibility. This allows teams to work together cohesively, leading to increased productivity and success.

However, open communication and transparency should not be mistaken for a license to be blunt or insensitive. It is crucial to practice empathy and mindfulness in our communication. By being mindful of our words and the impact they may have on others, we can ensure that our honesty is delivered with kindness and compassion.

In conclusion, open communication and transparency are indispensable elements in leading a meaningful and fulfilling life. By embracing honesty, we establish trust, build strong relationships, and create opportunities for personal growth. Whether in our personal or professional lives, the importance of being honest cannot be understated. Let us strive to communicate openly, transparently, and with empathy, as we embark on our journey towards a more genuine and fulfilling existence.

Healing from Betrayal and Rebuilding Trust

Betrayal is a deeply painful experience that can leave us feeling hurt, angry, and mistrustful. Whether it comes from a close friend, a romantic partner, or even a family member, the act of betrayal can shatter our sense of security and belief in others. However, healing from betrayal is not impossible. With time, effort, and a commitment to rebuilding trust, we can overcome the pain and create stronger, more meaningful relationships.

The process of healing begins with acknowledging and understanding our emotions. It is important to give ourselves permission to feel the pain and anger that betrayal brings. By allowing ourselves to grieve and process these emotions, we can start to move towards forgiveness and healing. It may also be helpful to seek support from trusted friends, family members, or even a therapist who can provide guidance and validation during this challenging time.

Rebuilding trust after betrayal requires open and honest communication. Both parties involved must be willing to confront the issue head-on, express their feelings, and listen to each other with empathy and compassion. Transparency is key in this process. It is essential for the person who betrayed to take responsibility for their actions, show genuine remorse, and make a sincere effort to make amends.

In order to rebuild trust, it is crucial to set boundaries and establish clear expectations. This may involve creating new agreements or guidelines for the relationship moving forward. Consistency in behavior and actions is vital to regaining trust. The person who was betrayed may need time and space to heal, and it is important for the person who betrayed to be patient and understanding during this process.

Rebuilding trust also requires a commitment to personal growth and development. Both parties must be willing to reflect on their own behaviors and make positive changes. This may involve addressing any underlying issues or patterns that contributed to the betrayal. By actively working on personal growth and self-improvement, individuals can create a solid foundation for a healthier, more honest relationship.

Ultimately, healing from betrayal and rebuilding trust is a journey that takes time, effort, and patience. It requires vulnerability and a willingness to be open to the possibility of being hurt again. However, by embracing forgiveness, honest communication, and personal growth, we can overcome the pain of betrayal and create relationships built on a foundation of trust and authenticity.

Remember, healing from betrayal is not just about repairing the relationship with the person who betrayed us. It is also about healing ourselves, learning from the experience, and growing into stronger, more resilient individuals. By doing so, we can move forward with the knowledge that honesty and trust are the cornerstones of a meaningful and fulfilling life.

Honesty in Friendships and Social Connections

Friendships and social connections are an integral part of our lives. They provide us with support, comfort, and a sense of belonging. But have you ever stopped to think about the role honesty plays in these relationships? Honesty is the foundation upon which all meaningful and fulfilling friendships are built. It is the cornerstone of trust, authenticity, and genuine connection. In this subchapter, we will explore the importance of honesty in friendships and social connections and how it can enhance our overall well-being.

Firstly, honesty fosters trust. When we are honest with our friends and social connections, we create an environment where trust can flourish. Trust forms the basis of any strong relationship, enabling us to rely on one another, confide in each other, and feel secure. Without honesty, trust becomes fragile, and the foundation of the friendship can crumble.

Moreover, honesty promotes authenticity. In a world where we often feel pressured to conform or wear masks, genuine connections can be hard to come by. However, when we are honest with ourselves and others, we allow our true selves to shine through. Authenticity attracts like-minded individuals who appreciate us for who we truly are, fostering deeper and more meaningful friendships.

Being honest in friendships and social connections also paves the way for growth and self-improvement. Honest feedback from trusted friends can help us recognize our blind spots, challenge our limiting beliefs, and encourage personal development. By embracing honesty, we create an open space for growth, as we learn from one another and strive to become the best versions of ourselves.

Additionally, honesty cultivates empathy and compassion. When we are honest about our thoughts, feelings, and experiences, we invite others to do the same. This vulnerability allows us to understand one another on a deeper level, fostering empathy and compassion. Through honest communication, we can support and uplift each other in times of need, creating a strong support system that enriches our lives.

In conclusion, honesty is the cornerstone of all meaningful and fulfilling friendships and social connections. By being honest with ourselves and others, we foster trust, authenticity, growth, and empathy. In a world where superficial connections and facades are prevalent, the importance of honesty cannot be overstated. Embrace honesty in your friendships and social connections, and witness the transformation it brings to your relationships and overall well-being.

Authenticity and Genuine Connections

In a world filled with superficial interactions and constant distractions, the value of authenticity and genuine connections cannot be overstated. In this subchapter, we will explore the significance of being honest in our relationships and how it forms the foundation for a meaningful and fulfilling life.

Being honest is not just about telling the truth; it is about being true to ourselves and others. When we live authentically, we align our thoughts, words, and actions, allowing our true selves to shine through. This authenticity attracts like-minded individuals who appreciate and value us for who we truly are. Genuine connections are established when we remove the masks we wear and present ourselves vulnerably and honestly to others.

Authenticity breeds trust, which is the cornerstone of any successful relationship. When we are honest with others, it creates a safe space for open communication and fosters a sense of security. Trust allows us to be our most authentic selves, knowing that we won't be judged or rejected. Genuine connections thrive in an environment of trust, deepening bonds and fostering emotional intimacy.

Furthermore, being honest helps us cultivate a deeper understanding of ourselves and others. When we are authentic in our interactions, we encourage others to do the same. This openness leads to meaningful conversations where we can explore our fears, desires, and vulnerabilities. Through these deep connections, we gain insight into our own values and beliefs, as well as those of others, broadening our perspectives and enriching our lives.

Living an honest life also frees us from the burden of deceit. When we are true to ourselves and others, we no longer need to keep up appearances or pretend to be someone we're not. This liberation allows us to focus on what truly matters – our genuine connections and personal growth.

In conclusion, authenticity and genuine connections are essential for a meaningful and fulfilling life. Being honest not only fosters trust and deepens relationships, but it also helps us understand ourselves and others on a deeper level. By embracing authenticity, we create an environment where everyone can be their true selves, forming connections that are built on trust and mutual understanding. Let us strive to be honest, not only in our words but in our actions, and experience the transformative power of authenticity in our lives.

Navigating Difficult Conversations

Difficult conversations are an inevitable part of life. Whether it's addressing a sensitive topic with a loved one, discussing a challenging issue at work, or confronting a friend about a problem, these conversations can often be anxiety-inducing and emotionally charged. However, learning how to navigate these difficult conversations is essential for personal growth and maintaining healthy relationships.

The importance of being honest extends beyond simply telling the truth. It involves effectively communicating our thoughts, feelings, and needs while also being receptive to those of others. When engaged in difficult conversations, honesty is the foundation on which understanding, trust, and resolution can be built.

One key aspect of navigating difficult conversations is to approach them with empathy and understanding. Recognizing that everyone has their own perspectives, experiences, and emotions can help create a safe space for open dialogue. Listening actively and without judgment is crucial, as it allows us to truly comprehend the other person's viewpoint, even if we may not agree with it. By practicing empathy, we can foster mutual respect and establish a foundation for productive conversation.

Another important skill to master is effective communication. Clearly expressing our thoughts and feelings while using "I" statements can prevent misunderstandings and defensiveness. It is important to avoid blaming or accusing the other person, as this can escalate tension and hinder progress. Instead, focus on using language that conveys your concerns and invites collaboration. Remember, the goal is not to win an argument but to find a solution or understanding that benefits everyone involved.

During difficult conversations, emotions can run high, making it challenging to stay calm and composed. However, managing emotions is crucial in order to maintain a respectful and productive dialogue. Taking deep breaths, allowing pauses, and practicing self-awareness can help regulate emotions and prevent impulsive reactions. Remember, honest conversations are not about suppressing emotions but expressing them in a constructive manner.

Lastly, it is important to be open to feedback and willing to compromise. Difficult conversations are opportunities for growth, and it's essential to be receptive to constructive criticism and alternative solutions. Be willing to find common ground or explore win-win outcomes that meet the needs of all parties involved.

In conclusion, navigating difficult conversations requires honesty, empathy, effective communication, emotional regulation, and a willingness to compromise. By approaching these conversations with the goal of understanding and finding mutually beneficial solutions, we can foster meaningful and fulfilling relationships while enhancing personal growth. Remember, difficult conversations can be challenging, but they also offer the opportunity for growth and deeper connections. Embrace them with honesty and openness, and you will pave the way for a more meaningful and fulfilling life.

Honesty in Professional Relationships

In today's fast-paced and competitive world, the importance of honesty in professional relationships cannot be overstated. Whether you are an employee, a manager, an entrepreneur, or a freelancer, integrity and trustworthiness are fundamental qualities that can set you apart and pave the way for long-term success.

At its core, honesty in professional relationships encompasses open communication, transparency, and a commitment to ethical behavior. When you prioritize honesty in your interactions with colleagues, superiors, clients, and business partners, you foster an environment of trust and collaboration. It lays the foundation for meaningful connections and paves the way for genuine growth and progress.

One key aspect of honesty in professional relationships is being truthful about your capabilities and limitations. It is tempting to overpromise and exaggerate your skills in order to win contracts or impress others, but this approach is short-sighted and can lead to disappointment and damaged relationships in the long run. By being honest about what you can and cannot deliver, you build credibility and demonstrate integrity, earning the respect and trust of those you work with.

Furthermore, honesty in professional relationships also involves giving credit where it is due. Acknowledge the contributions of your team members and colleagues, and avoid taking credit for their work. This not only fosters a positive and collaborative work environment but also establishes a reputation as someone who values fairness and recognizes the efforts of others.

Another crucial aspect of honesty in professional relationships is admitting mistakes and taking responsibility. We are all human, and errors are bound to happen. However, instead of hiding or deflecting blame, owning up to your mistakes demonstrates accountability and a commitment to learning and growing. By doing so, you not only cultivate trust but also promote a culture of honesty and continuous improvement within your professional circle.

Moreover, being honest in professional relationships also means being a reliable and consistent communicator. Responding promptly to emails, following through on commitments, and providing updates when necessary are all essential elements of building trust and maintaining strong connections. When others know they can rely on you for honest and timely communication, it creates a sense of dependability and professionalism.

In conclusion, honesty is the backbone of successful professional relationships. By prioritizing integrity, transparency, and ethical behavior, you can build trust, credibility, and lasting connections with your colleagues, clients, and business partners. Whether you are just starting out in your career or are a seasoned professional, embracing honesty will not only contribute to your personal growth but also create a more fulfilling and meaningful professional life for yourself and those around you.

Integrity and Ethical Decision-Making

In a world that often seems to prioritize personal gain and success over honesty and morality, it is crucial to understand the importance of integrity and ethical decision-making. These values form the bedrock of our character and have a profound impact on our lives and the lives of those around us. In this subchapter, we delve deep into the significance of being honest and how it can contribute to a meaningful and fulfilling life.

Integrity, at its core, means being true to oneself and acting in accordance with one's values and principles. It involves consistently aligning our thoughts, words, and actions with what we believe to be right and just. When we possess integrity, we become individuals who can be trusted and relied upon. Our relationships flourish, and our reputation stands strong, as people recognize and respect our commitment to honesty.

Ethical decision-making is closely intertwined with integrity. It involves the conscious evaluation of the potential consequences of our choices and considering the moral implications. By consistently making ethical decisions, we create a positive ripple effect in our lives and the world. Our actions become a reflection of our values, and we inspire others to do the same, fostering a culture of integrity and honesty.

Being honest is not always easy, especially when faced with difficult circumstances or the temptation to take shortcuts. However, the benefits of honesty far outweigh any momentary gains. Honesty builds trust, deepens relationships, and enhances our personal growth. It allows us to live with integrity, knowing that we have acted in accordance with our values and can face ourselves in the mirror without guilt or regret.

Living a meaningful and fulfilling life is intricately tied to our ability to be honest. When we are honest with ourselves and others, we create authenticity and genuine connections. We foster a sense of purpose and fulfillment, as our actions align with our beliefs. Honesty empowers us to make choices that contribute to our personal growth and happiness, rather than being driven solely by external expectations or desires.

In conclusion, integrity and ethical decision-making form the foundation for a meaningful and fulfilling life. By embracing honesty, we cultivate trust, build strong relationships, and foster a sense of purpose. It is through our commitment to honesty that we can truly live a life that is authentic, genuine, and in alignment with our values. Let us strive to be individuals of integrity, making ethical decisions that positively impact ourselves and the world around us.

Establishing Trust with Colleagues and Superiors

Trust is the cornerstone of any successful professional relationship. Whether you are working with colleagues or superiors, establishing trust is crucial for a harmonious and productive workplace environment. In this subchapter, we will explore the importance of being honest and how it can help you build trust with those around you.

Honesty is not only a virtue but also a powerful tool that can transform your professional life. When you are transparent and truthful in your interactions, you create a foundation of trust that can lead to increased collaboration, effective communication, and enhanced productivity.

When it comes to your colleagues, being honest allows for open and authentic relationships. By expressing your thoughts and opinions sincerely, you encourage others to do the same. This fosters an environment where ideas can be freely shared, leading to innovation and problem-solving. Honesty also helps build a sense of camaraderie and teamwork, as people feel comfortable relying on one another.

Similarly, establishing trust with your superiors is vital for career advancement. Honest communication with your boss allows for a transparent understanding of your abilities, goals, and aspirations. By being open about your strengths and weaknesses, you enable your superiors to provide you with the necessary guidance and support to grow professionally. Trustworthy employees are often entrusted with more responsibilities and opportunities for career advancement.

Being honest also means admitting mistakes and taking ownership of them. When you make a mistake, it is crucial to acknowledge it instead of trying to cover it up. This demonstrates integrity and accountability, which are highly valued traits in any professional setting. By taking responsibility for your actions, you not only earn the respect of your colleagues and superiors but also foster an environment where learning from mistakes is encouraged.

In an era where trust is often questioned, being honest can set you apart from the competition. It builds credibility, enhances your reputation, and establishes you as a reliable and trustworthy professional. People are more likely to seek your opinion, rely on your expertise, and value your contributions when they know they can trust you.

In conclusion, establishing trust with colleagues and superiors is vital for a meaningful and fulfilling professional life. By being honest, you create an environment conducive to collaboration, open communication, and personal growth. Honesty builds credibility, fosters teamwork, and enhances your reputation. Embracing honesty as a core value will not only benefit your career but also lead to a more fulfilling and satisfying professional journey.

Chapter 5: Honesty as a Lifestyle Choice

The Ripple Effect of Honesty

In our fast-paced and often unpredictable world, honesty seems to be a rare commodity. It is often overshadowed by deceit, manipulation, and the pursuit of personal gain. However, honesty is not just a virtue; it is the foundation for a meaningful and fulfilling life. Its impact extends far beyond our immediate actions and has a powerful ripple effect on both ourselves and those around us.

At its core, honesty is about aligning our thoughts, words, and actions with integrity. When we choose to be honest, we establish a strong sense of trust and credibility. This is crucial in all aspects of life, whether it be personal relationships, professional endeavors, or even our own self-worth. When we are honest, we build authentic connections with others, fostering deeper and more meaningful relationships.

The ripple effect of honesty goes beyond individual interactions. When we choose to live a life of honesty, we inspire others to do the same. People often look up to those who display integrity and honesty, and in turn, they are more likely to mirror these qualities. By being honest, we become role models for others, setting a positive example and encouraging a culture of honesty and transparency.

Furthermore, the impact of honesty can extend to the wider community and society as a whole. When honesty becomes the norm, it fosters an environment of trust and cooperation. People feel safe and secure when they can rely on the honesty of others. This leads to healthier relationships, stronger communities, and a more harmonious society.

On a personal level, honesty brings immense liberation and peace of mind. Living a life of honesty means that we no longer need to hide behind a façade or keep secrets. We can be our true selves, embracing our strengths and accepting our flaws. Honesty allows us to live authentically, leading to a greater sense of self-acceptance and contentment.

In conclusion, the ripple effect of honesty cannot be understated. Its impact radiates beyond our immediate actions, influencing both individuals and society as a whole. By choosing to be honest, we not only cultivate stronger relationships and inspire others, but we also experience personal growth and fulfillment. Let us embrace honesty as the foundation for a meaningful and fulfilling life, and witness the positive ripple effect it creates in every aspect of our lives.

Inspiring Others through Honesty

Honesty is not just a virtue that benefits us individually; it has the power to inspire and transform the lives of those around us. When we embrace honesty as the foundation of our interactions, we become beacons of integrity, shining a light on the importance of being honest and encouraging others to do the same. This subchapter aims to explore the ways in which we can inspire others through our own commitment to honesty, ultimately fostering a more meaningful and fulfilling life for everyone.

One of the most profound impacts of being honest is the trust it builds among individuals. When we consistently display honesty in our words and actions, we create an environment of trustworthiness. Others feel safe and secure knowing that they can rely on us and confide in us without fear of deceit or betrayal. This trust serves as a catalyst, inspiring them to adopt a similar approach and nurturing a culture of honesty in all their relationships.

Furthermore, when we choose honesty, we become role models for those around us. Our commitment to truthfulness demonstrates the courage and strength it takes to be honest, even in challenging situations. By sharing our experiences and the positive outcomes that honesty has brought into our lives, we inspire others to embrace this virtue as well. Our honesty becomes contagious, spreading a ripple effect of integrity throughout our community.

In addition to cultivating trust and serving as role models, inspiring others through honesty involves creating a safe and supportive space for open communication. When we are honest, we encourage others to express their thoughts and emotions freely, knowing that their words will be met with understanding and respect. By listening attentively and responding with empathy, we inspire others to share their own truths, fostering deeper connections and nurturing personal growth.

Ultimately, inspiring others through honesty is a powerful way to contribute to the greater good. When we prioritize honesty in our interactions, we contribute to a society built on trust, authenticity, and mutual respect. We become catalysts for positive change, inspiring others to embrace honesty as a means to lead more meaningful and fulfilling lives.

In conclusion, the importance of being honest cannot be overstated. By embodying honesty in our own lives and inspiring others to do the same, we create an environment where trust flourishes, role models are born, and open communication thrives. Through our commitment to honesty, we have the power to inspire others and contribute to a society built on integrity, ultimately leading to a more meaningful and fulfilling life for everyone.

Contributing to an Honest Society

In a world where deception and dishonesty seem to be rampant, it is crucial for each one of us to reflect on the importance of being honest and consider how we can contribute to creating an honest society. Honesty is not just a virtue; it is the foundation for a meaningful and fulfilling life. This subchapter aims to shed light on the significance of honesty and provide actionable steps for every individual to contribute to building a more honest society.

First and foremost, honesty is vital because it forms the basis of trust. Trust is the glue that holds relationships, communities, and even nations together. Without trust, there can be no genuine connections, cooperation, or progress. By being honest in our words, actions, and intentions, we foster an environment of trust and reliability, enabling healthy relationships to flourish.

Moreover, honesty allows us to align our actions with our values. When we choose to be honest, we are living authentically, staying true to ourselves and our principles. This alignment not only brings inner peace and self-respect but also inspires others to do the same. By leading by example and being honest, we encourage those around us to embrace honesty as well.

To contribute to an honest society, we must start by cultivating self-awareness. This involves reflecting on our own tendency to be dishonest, whether it be through little white lies or more significant ethical lapses. Recognizing our own weaknesses in this area enables us to work on them and strive for personal growth. By continuously striving to be more honest, we set a positive example for others and contribute to a culture of integrity.

Additionally, we can encourage honesty by promoting open dialogue and creating a safe space for truth-telling. By fostering an environment where people feel comfortable expressing their thoughts and emotions honestly, we create opportunities for genuine communication and understanding. Encouraging active listening, empathy, and non-judgmental attitudes can further facilitate honest interactions.

Finally, education plays a crucial role in shaping an honest society. By teaching the importance of honesty from an early age, we can instill values that will guide individuals throughout their lives. Schools, families, and communities should emphasize the significance of honesty and provide resources to help individuals navigate ethical dilemmas. Education can empower individuals to make ethical choices and take responsibility for their actions, thereby contributing to a more honest society.

In conclusion, honesty is not only essential for personal growth and fulfillment but also for building a society based on trust, authenticity, and integrity. By cultivating self-awareness, promoting open dialogue, and emphasizing the importance of honesty through education, each one of us has the power to contribute to an honest society. Let us strive to be beacons of honesty and inspire others to join us on this transformative journey towards a more meaningful and fulfilling life.

Overcoming the Temptations of Dishonesty

In today's fast-paced and highly competitive world, the temptation to be dishonest can be overwhelming. Whether it's in business, relationships, or personal endeavors, the lure of taking shortcuts or bending the truth can seem like a quick and easy way to get ahead. However, the book "Honesty: The Foundation for a Meaningful and Fulfilling Life" strongly emphasizes the importance of being honest and the long-term benefits it brings.

One of the key challenges we all face is resisting the allure of dishonesty. It's human nature to want to avoid negative consequences or to achieve success at any cost. However, dishonesty often comes with a heavy price tag. It erodes trust, damages relationships, and tarnishes one's reputation. In contrast, honesty builds trust, strengthens bonds, and cultivates a sense of integrity that is essential for a meaningful and fulfilling life.

So how can we overcome the temptations of dishonesty? The first step is to recognize that honesty is not just a moral virtue but also a practical one. Being honest saves us from the constant anxiety and fear of being caught in a lie. It liberates us from the burden of deception and allows us to live authentically. By embracing honesty, we create a solid foundation upon which we can build our lives.

Another important aspect to consider is the power of self-reflection. Taking a moment to pause and reflect on our actions and intentions can help us understand the underlying reasons behind our temptations to be dishonest. Are we driven by fear, insecurity, or the desire for immediate gratification? By recognizing these inner motivations, we can address them head-on and find healthier ways to meet our needs without compromising our integrity.

Surrounding ourselves with the right influences is also crucial. We are greatly influenced by the people we spend time with, so it's vital to choose friends and mentors who value honesty and integrity. By associating with individuals who prioritize these values, we are more likely to be inspired and encouraged to stay true to ourselves.

Lastly, practicing honesty in small, everyday situations can strengthen our ability to resist the temptations of dishonesty. Honesty is a habit that can be cultivated, and each time we choose to be truthful, we reinforce our commitment to living a meaningful and fulfilling life.

In conclusion, overcoming the temptations of dishonesty is a continuous journey that requires self-awareness, reflection, and the conscious choice to prioritize honesty. By embracing honesty as the foundation of our lives, we can build stronger relationships, earn the trust of others, and ultimately achieve a more meaningful and fulfilling existence.

Recognizing the Consequences

In our journey towards leading a meaningful and fulfilling life, one of the crucial pillars that we need to strengthen is honesty. Honesty forms the bedrock of our character and shapes our interactions with the world around us. It is a virtue that holds immense importance, not just in personal relationships, but also in professional settings and society at large.

However, being honest goes beyond just telling the truth. It also means recognizing and understanding the consequences that come with our actions, words, and decisions. This subchapter delves into the significance of recognizing these consequences and how they shape our lives.

When we act with honesty, we are more likely to experience positive consequences. Honesty fosters trust and strengthens relationships, enabling us to build meaningful connections with others. By recognizing the consequences of our actions, we can maintain the trust and respect of those around us, which in turn leads to a more fulfilling life.

On the other hand, when we are dishonest, the consequences can be detrimental. Lying, cheating, or deceiving others might seem like an easy way out in the short term, but it erodes trust and damages relationships. The consequences of dishonesty can haunt us for years to come, causing guilt, regret, and even the loss of valuable connections.

Recognizing the consequences of our actions also helps us make better decisions. When we are aware of the potential outcomes, we can weigh the impact and choose the path that aligns with our values and goals. By understanding that our choices have far-reaching consequences, we become more accountable for our behavior and make choices that contribute to our personal growth and the well-being of those around us.

Moreover, recognizing the consequences of dishonesty in society is equally important. When we understand the negative ramifications of dishonesty on a larger scale, we can actively work towards creating a more honest and trustworthy society. By setting an example through our own honest actions, we inspire others to do the same, creating a ripple effect that can bring about positive change.

In conclusion, recognizing the consequences of our actions, words, and decisions is an essential aspect of leading an honest and meaningful life. By understanding the impact of our honesty, we can build and nurture strong relationships, make better choices, and contribute to the creation of a more trustworthy society. Let us embrace the power of recognizing the consequences as we strive towards living a life filled with integrity and fulfillment.

Developing a Strong Moral Compass

Honesty: The Foundation for a Meaningful and Fulfilling Life

In a world full of distractions and temptations, it is crucial to develop a strong moral compass that guides us in making honest choices. Honesty is not just about telling the truth; it is about living a life of integrity and authenticity. In this subchapter, we will explore the significance of being honest and how it can transform our lives for the better.

The importance of being honest cannot be overstated. When we are honest, we build trust with others, maintain strong relationships, and foster a sense of self-respect. Honesty is the pillar upon which all other virtues are built. It is the key to living a meaningful and fulfilling life.

Being honest starts with ourselves. We must first acknowledge our own flaws and weaknesses. By being honest with ourselves, we can grow, learn, and improve as individuals. It is only when we are honest with ourselves that we can be honest with others.

When we are honest, we attract like-minded individuals into our lives. We surround ourselves with people who value integrity and authenticity. Honesty creates a positive ripple effect that spreads throughout our personal and professional relationships. It cultivates an environment of trust, open communication, and respect.

Developing a strong moral compass requires us to make conscious choices. We must consistently evaluate our actions and ensure they align with our values. This means standing up for what is right, even when it is difficult or inconvenient. It means taking responsibility for our mistakes and making amends when necessary.

To strengthen our moral compass, it is essential to seek out role models who embody honesty. These individuals can inspire and guide us on our journey towards becoming more honest. We can learn from their experiences, values, and principles.

In conclusion, developing a strong moral compass is vital for leading a meaningful and fulfilling life. Honesty forms the bedrock of our character, guiding our choices and actions. By being honest with ourselves and others, we build trust, maintain strong relationships, and foster personal growth. Let us strive to develop a strong moral compass, embracing honesty as the foundation for a life well-lived.

Honesty and a Fulfilling Life

In today's fast-paced and constantly evolving world, it is easy to get caught up in the hustle and bustle, often overlooking the significance of one simple virtue - honesty. Honesty is not only about telling the truth; it is a fundamental principle that lays the foundation for a meaningful and fulfilling life. Regardless of our background, profession, or personal beliefs, honesty is something that resonates with everyone.

The importance of being honest cannot be overstated. It is the key that unlocks the door to trust, integrity, and authenticity. When we are honest with ourselves and others, we build solid relationships that are based on transparency and openness. This not only fosters stronger connections with our loved ones but also paves the way for success in both personal and professional endeavors.

Living an honest life means not only speaking the truth but also acting with integrity in all aspects of life. It means making choices based on moral values rather than personal gain. When we prioritize honesty, we become accountable for our actions, and this cultivates a sense of self-respect and dignity. By embracing honesty, we empower ourselves to become better individuals and make a positive impact on the world around us.

Furthermore, honesty plays a vital role in personal growth and self-discovery. It allows us to confront our weaknesses and acknowledge our mistakes, leading to learning and self-improvement. By being honest with ourselves, we can identify areas for development and take the necessary steps to become the best version of ourselves. This path of self-discovery ultimately leads to fulfillment and a greater sense of purpose in life.

In a society where deception and dishonesty are often glamorized, it is crucial to remind ourselves of the value of honesty. Honesty is the cornerstone of trust, respect, and meaningful relationships. It is the glue that holds individuals and communities together. By embracing honesty as a way of life, we not only create a positive impact on our own lives but also contribute to a more honest and compassionate world.

In conclusion, honesty is not just a virtue; it is the foundation for a meaningful and fulfilling life. It is a guiding principle that allows us to build trust, cultivate integrity, and embark on a path of self-discovery. Regardless of our backgrounds or beliefs, honesty resonates with everyone. By prioritizing honesty in our thoughts, words, and actions, we can unlock a life filled with purpose, joy, and authentic connections. Let honesty be the compass that guides us towards a brighter future, both individually and collectively.

Finding Meaning and Purpose

Subchapter: Finding Meaning and Purpose

In our journey through life, we often find ourselves questioning the purpose and meaning behind our existence. It is a search that transcends age, gender, and cultural backgrounds. We all crave a sense of fulfillment and significance in our lives. But where do we find it? How can we unlock the door to a meaningful and purposeful existence?

The answer lies in honesty. Honesty is not just about being truthful with others; it is also about being true to ourselves. When we live in alignment with our values and principles, we create a solid foundation for a meaningful and fulfilling life.

Honesty allows us to understand ourselves better. By examining our thoughts, actions, and motivations, we gain insight into who we truly are. This self-awareness is the first step towards finding our purpose. When we are honest with ourselves, we can identify our passions, strengths, and values, and align them with our actions. This alignment brings a sense of purpose to our lives.

Being honest also fosters authenticity. When we are true to ourselves, we can show up as our genuine selves in all areas of life - relationships, work, and personal pursuits. This authenticity attracts like-minded individuals and opportunities that resonate with who we truly are. It allows us to build meaningful connections and engage in activities that bring us joy and fulfillment.

Moreover, honesty cultivates a sense of integrity. When we are honest, we have nothing to hide. We can stand tall, knowing that our actions align with our values. This integrity provides a strong sense of self-worth and self-respect. It allows us to navigate life's challenges with grace and resilience, knowing that we are living a life of purpose and meaning.

In our quest for meaning and purpose, it is essential to recognize the importance of being honest. By embracing honesty as a guiding principle, we embark on a transformative journey of self-discovery. We gain clarity about our passions, values, and strengths, and we align them with our actions. This alignment creates authenticity and integrity, paving the way for a meaningful and fulfilling life.

So, let us embark on this journey of honesty, for it is the foundation upon which we can build a life of purpose, significance, and true fulfillment.

Cultivating Gratitude and Authentic Happiness

In today's fast-paced world, it is easy to get caught up in the hustle and bustle of everyday life. We often find ourselves striving for more, constantly seeking happiness and fulfillment in external achievements and possessions. However, what if the key to true happiness and a meaningful life lies not in materialistic pursuits, but in cultivating gratitude and authenticity?

Gratitude is a powerful practice that can transform our lives. By consciously acknowledging and appreciating the blessings and positive aspects of our lives, we shift our focus from what we lack to what we have. This shift in perspective allows us to experience a deep sense of contentment and fulfillment, even in the face of challenges.

Cultivating gratitude begins with a simple shift in mindset. Instead of taking things for granted, we learn to recognize and cherish the small joys and blessings that surround us daily. This could be as simple as expressing gratitude for a delicious meal, a beautiful sunset, or a kind gesture from a loved one. By practicing gratitude regularly, we train our minds to focus on the positive, fostering a sense of abundance and appreciation for life's blessings.

Authentic happiness, on the other hand, stems from living a life aligned with our values and true selves. It is about being honest with ourselves and others, and living in alignment with our core beliefs and principles. When we live authentically, we experience a deep sense of fulfillment and joy, as we are no longer trying to fit into societal expectations or chasing external validation.

Being honest with ourselves and others is not always easy. It requires self-reflection, introspection, and the willingness to confront our fears and insecurities. However, the rewards of living an authentic life are immeasurable. When we are true to ourselves, we attract genuine connections and experiences that align with our values, leading to a more meaningful and fulfilling existence.

In conclusion, cultivating gratitude and authentic happiness are essential components of leading a meaningful and fulfilling life. By practicing gratitude, we shift our focus towards the positive and experience a deep sense of contentment. Living authentically, on the other hand, allows us to align our actions with our values, leading to a greater sense of fulfillment and joy. So, let us embark on this journey towards gratitude and authenticity, and discover the transformative power they hold in our lives.